— MAKE —
THE OFFICE
GREAT AGAIN

90+ REASONS WORKING AT THE OFFICE TRUMPS REMOTE WORK

CREATED BY OSCAR BERG
oscarberg.net

ILLUSTRATIONS BY LEREMY GAN
leremy.com

PUBLISHER: Gr8 Mountains AB, Lund, Sweden
PRINT: BoD — Books on Demand, Norderstedt, Germany
ISBN: 978-91-988415-3-4

#MOGA

JOIN A PROGRESSIVE MOVEMENT THAT AIMS TO REINSTATE THE OFFICE AS THE PLACE WHERE ALL WORK HAPPENS

THE DAILY COMMUTE

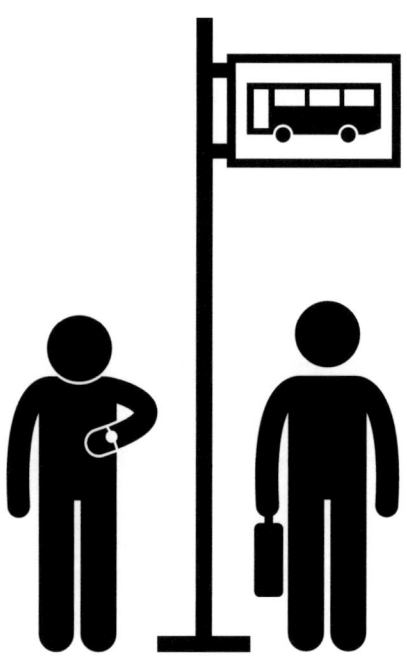

**COMMUTING IS THE EASIEST WAY TO WASTE
LEISURE TIME YOU DON'T REALLY NEED**

THE RENDEZVOUS

BY MAKING YOURSELF INVISIBLE YOU CAN AVOID ANY COLLEAGUES YOU SPOT ON YOUR COMMUTE

THE LIE-IN SUBSTITUTE

TAKE A NAP ON YOUR COMMUTE INSTEAD OF STAYING IN BED AND BEING LATE FOR WORK

OFFICE HOURS

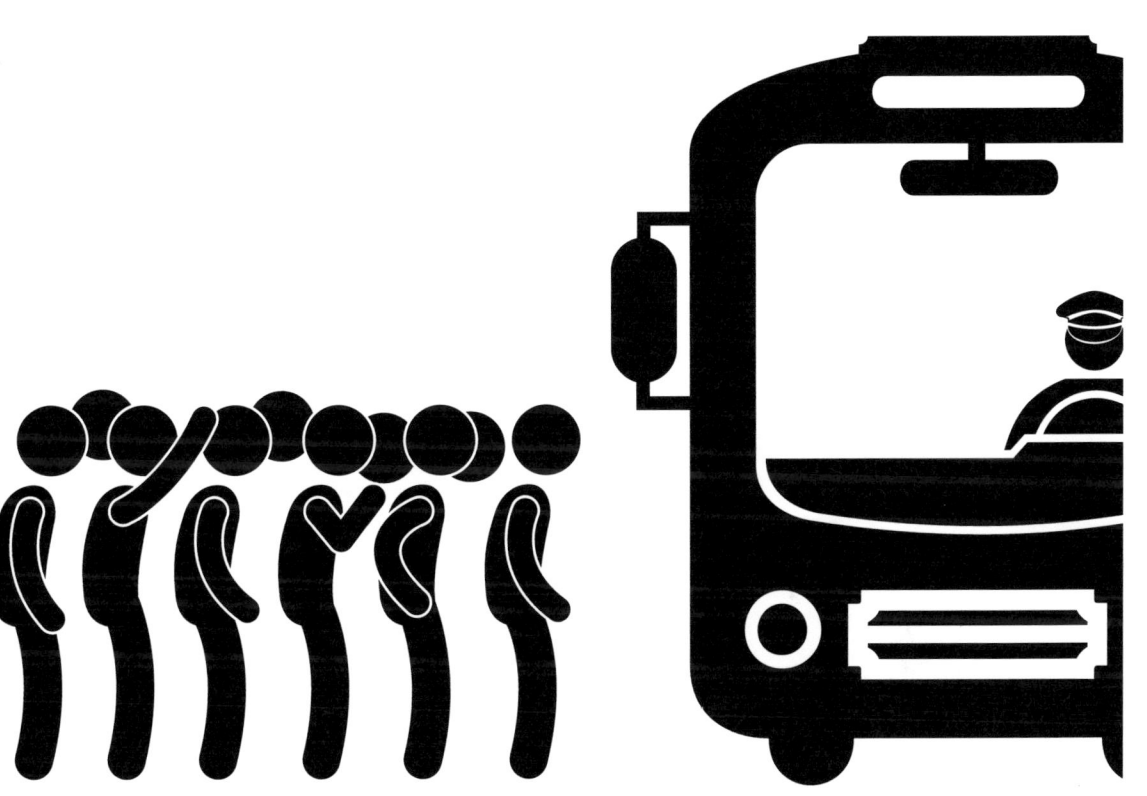

ENJOY THE COMPANY OF PERFECT STRANGERS WHEN COMMUTING – THE MORE THE MERRIER!

THE CARBON FOOTPRINT

**BE PART OF A MOVEMENT THAT WILL
FUNDAMENTALLY CHANGE THE FUTURE**

THE LOST UMBRELLA

IF IT RAINS, CHANCES ARE YOU'LL FIND AN UMBRELLA AT THE OFFICE THAT YOU CAN "BORROW"

THE TIME CLOCK

REMINDS YOU WHEN TO START AND STOP WORK

TOO FEW HOT DESKS

YOU JUST LOVED PLAYING MUSICAL CHAIRS
WHEN YOU WERE A KID, DIDN'T YOU?

OFFICE WIFI

MAKES YOU APPRECIATE YOUR EXPENSIVE
BUT SUPER-FAST BROADBAND AT HOME

MULTITASKING

**BY LOOKING BUSY YOU WILL BE THOUGHT IMPORTANT
AND THUS BE MORE SOUGHT-AFTER**

MASTER SUPPRESSION TECHNIQUES

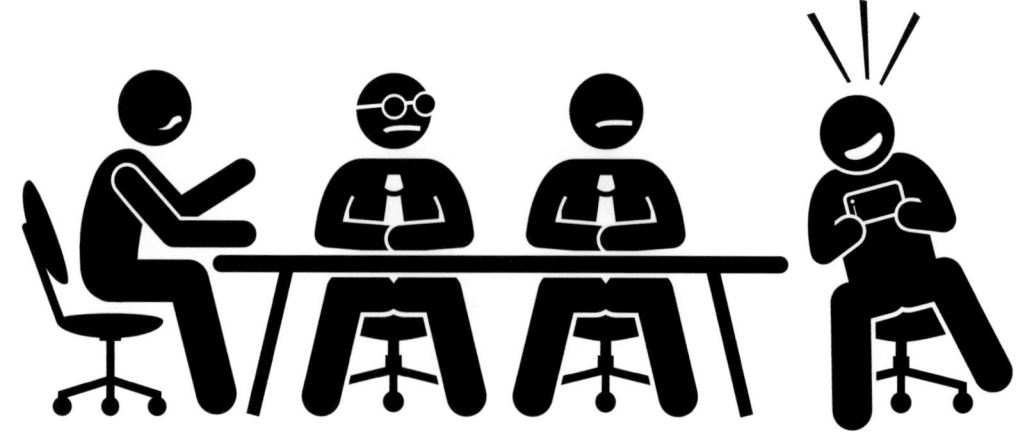

MAKES YOU FEEL LESS INFERIOR TO THOSE WHO ARE SMARTER THAN YOU

OFFICE COFFEE

KEEPS YOU FROM DRINKING TOO MUCH COFFEE

THE PAPER JAM

A PERFECT OPPORTUNITY TO PRACTISE MINDFULNESS

BRING YOUR OWN CAKE

**HELP YOUR COLLEAGUES
REMEMBER YOUR BIRTHDAY**

THE DRESS CODE

**KEEPS YOUR PERSONALITY FROM
BEING EXPOSED AT WORK**

CASUAL FRIDAY

**MAKES THE OFFICE FEEL LESS STIFF
EVERY ONCE IN A WHILE**

BAD HAIR DAY

**MAKES YOU ENVY ALL THE BALD
MEN AT THE OFFICE...NOT!**

THE "YOUR MOTHER DOESN'T WORK HERE" SIGN

REMINDS YOU TO CALL THE CLEANER TO CLEAN UP YOUR MESS

THE ACCESS CARD PHOTO

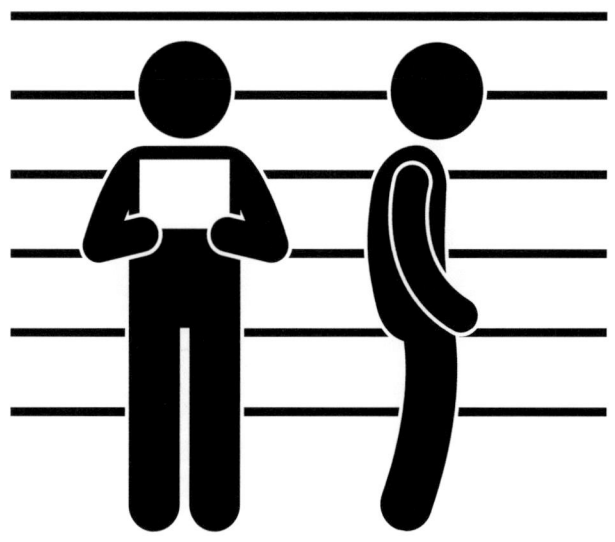

HELPS YOU REMEMBER HOW YOU FEEL ON REALLY BAD DAYS

OFFICE POLITICS

**GIVES YOU SOMETHING TO DO WHEN YOU'VE
LOST ALL INTEREST IN CREATING VALUE**

"WE ARE A FAMILY HERE"

BUILDS LOYALTY IN A LESS THREATENING WAY THAN "WE KNOW WHERE YOU LIVE"

MEETING ROOM VENTILATION

**HELPS YOU KEEP YOUR MEETINGS
SHORT AND EFFICIENT**

THE POINTLESS MEETING

Cute
cat

**KEEPS YOUR CHAIR WARM FOR
THE NEXT POINTLESS MEETING**

PEOPLE COMING IN SICK

**REMINDS YOU TO BUY ASPIRIN
AND NEW COVID TESTS**

MICROMANAGEMENT

MAKES YOUR BOSS FEEL NEEDED AGAIN
= THE PURPOSE OF YOUR EMPLOYMENT

THE OPEN OFFICE

GIVES YOU A CHANCE TO MAKE USE OF YOUR
NEW NOISE-CANCELLING HEADPHONES

EATING AT YOUR DESK

**ANOTHER GREAT OPPORTUNITY
TO PRACTISE MINDFULNESS**

TABLE FOOTBALL

**MAKES YOUR DULL, BORING WORKPLACE
SEEM ALMOST COOL AND FUN**

PRINTER RAGE

A SUBSTITUTE FOR TAKING OUT YOUR ANGER ON YOUR COLLEAGUES

ALL WORK & NO PLAY

HERE'S JOHNNY!

**SAVE ALL THE FUN FOR YOUR SPARE TIME
— IF YOU GET ANY, THAT IS**

WORKPLACE INEQUALITY

THIS CAN WORK OUT GREAT FOR YOU!

(DISCLAIMER: ONLY IF ARE A MAN)

THE BIG BOSS

BETTER THAN HAVING THE ALPHA MALES WREAKING HAVOC ON THE STREETS

THE MICROWAVED FISH LUNCH

A GOOD REASON TO GET OUT
AND GRAB SOME FRESH AIR

THE FORGOTTEN LUNCH BOX

**MIGHT JUST TURN OUT TO BE
"A DELIGHTFUL SURPRISE"**

OFFICE CONSTRUCTION WORK

GIVES YOU A VALID REASON FOR TAKING
A WELL-DESERVED BREAK

INVOLUNTARY EAVESDROPPING

MIGHT GIVE YOU A COMPETITIVE
EDGE OVER YOUR COLLEAGUES

CREATIVE SHOW-OFF

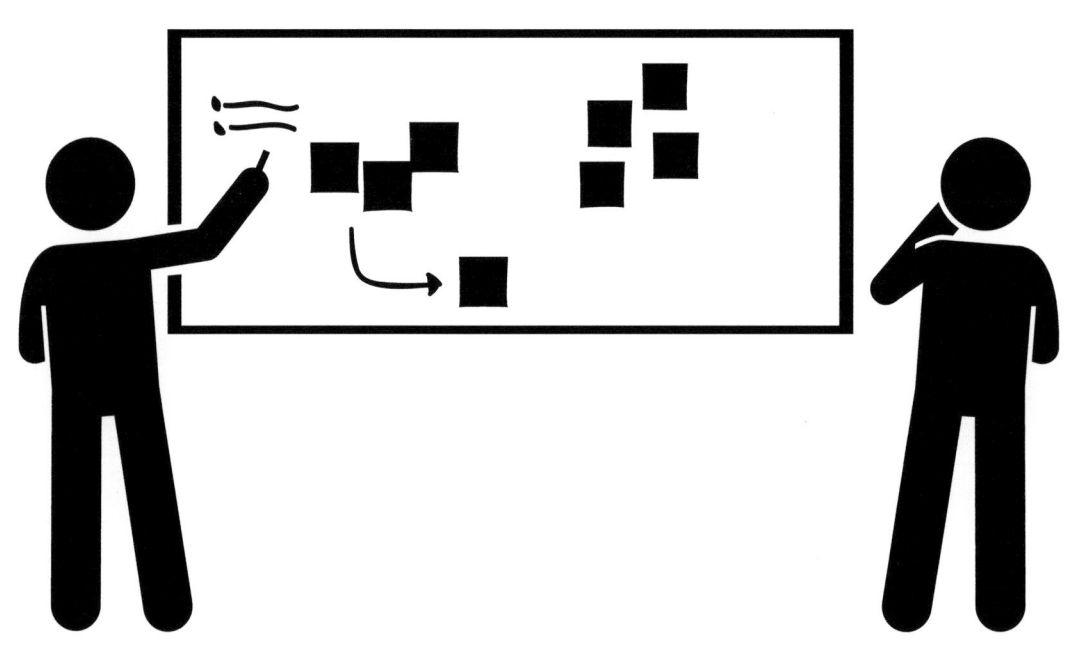

**STANDING BY THE WHITEBOARD WITH A PEN
WILL MAKE YOU LOOK CREATIVE**

THE PHYSICAL PRINTER QUEUE

THE OFFICE IS THE PERFECT PLACE WHEN YOU NEED TO PRINT OUT THE INTERNET

TIME-WASTING

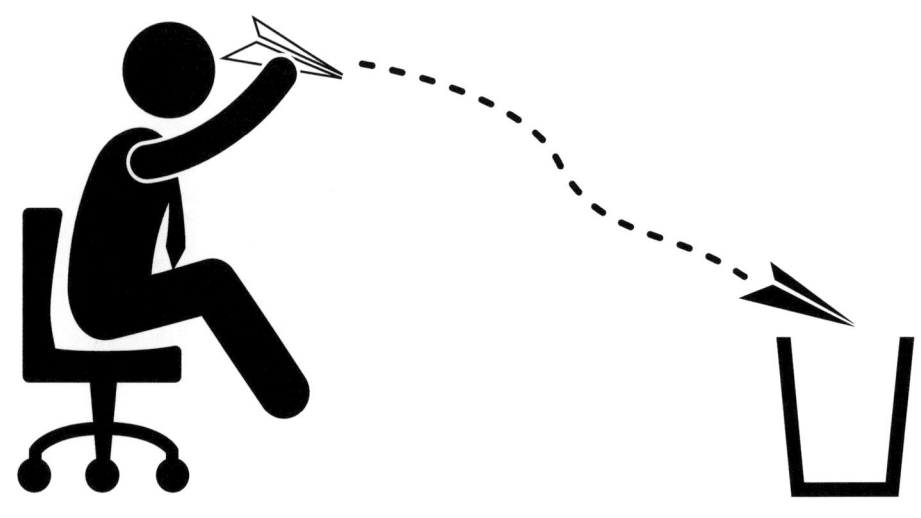

**HELPS YOU FILL YOUR 8 HOURS WHEN YOU
HAVE 2 HOURS' WORTH OF WORK A DAY**

THE OFFICE CUBICLE

**GIVES YOU THE OPPORTUNITY TO POP UP
OVER YOUR CUBICLE WALL UNANNOUNCED**

WATER COOLER TALK

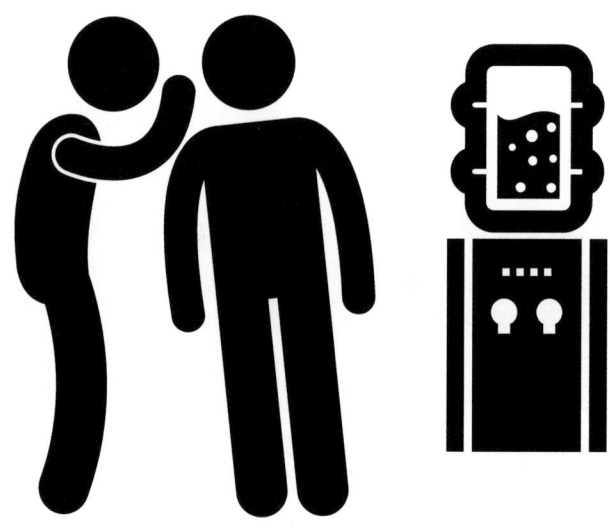

**PROVIDES AN EFFECTVE WAY TO SPREAD GOSSIP
ABOUT COLLEAGUES YOU DON'T LIKE**

THE "FULL" CALENDAR

NO ONE WILL QUESTION WHETHER YOU ARE BEING PRODUCTIVE

OFFICE PRANKS

**BE CERTAIN NO COLLEAGUE WILL EVER FEEL SAFE
(OR BE ABLE TO FOCUS) AT WORK**

THE FIXED WORK SCHEDULE

**UPSET YOUR COLLEAGUES
BY LEAVING EARLY**

THE HOVERING BOSS

**REMINDS YOU TO TAKE BREAKS WHEN
BINGE-WATCHING GAME OF THRONES**

THE SUGGESTION BOX

**MAKES YOUR BOSS HAPPY AS THEY CAN TAKE
CREDIT FOR YOUR ANONYMOUS IDEAS**

THE ANNOYING COLLEAGUE

MAKES SURE YOU VALUE ANY UNINTERRUPTED
WORK TIME YOU MIGHT GET

THE STOLEN MEETING ROOM

SAVES YOU FROM THE NEXT
POINTLESS MEETING

BACK-STABBING

HELPS YOU ADVANCE YOUR OWN CAREER
WITHOUT A LOT OF HARD WORK

FLUORESCENT LIGHTING

HELPS YOU BUILD EMPATHY FOR PEOPLE WORKING IN SWEATSHOPS

WORKPLACE SURVEILLANCE

**FACE IT, THIS IS THE ONLY WAY
YOUR BOSS IS GOING TO TRUST YOU**

THE MEETING THAT SHOULD HAVE BEEN AN EMAIL

MAKES TIME SEEM TO MOVE FASTER

SOUL-DESTROYING WORK

MAKES YOU LONG FOR THE DAY WHEN ARTIFICIAL INTELLIGENCE WILL TAKE OVER YOUR JOB

FORCED SYSTEM UPDATES

SAVES YOU FROM A LOT OF WORK

THE INTERNSHIP

SAVES YOU TIME AND ENERGY AS YOU DON'T NEED TO FETCH YOUR OWN COFFEE

THE DOUBLE-BOOKED MEETING ROOM

A DUEL TO THE DEATH
BRIGHTENS UP YOUR DAY

BRAYING MANAGERS

WHEN THEY SUCK THE OXYGEN OUT OF THE ROOM
THAT STIFF DRINK WILL BE MORE EFFECTIVE

THE OFFICE PARTY

IF YOU ARE LUCKY, YOU WILL BE ONE OF THE TEN
WHO GET FIRED AFTER AN OFFICE PARTY*

* according to research was carried out by AfterDrink.com

SITTING DOWN EQUALS WORKING

BEING SEATED MAKES YOUR BOSS THINK
YOU ARE BEING PRODUCTIVE

FACE TIME

GETS YOU SPECIAL TREATMENT JUST BY BEING
PHYSICALLY CLOSE TO YOUR BOSS

LOUD CONVERSATIONS

KEEPS YOUR COLLEAGUES (A.K.A. COMPETITORS) FROM DOING ANY MEANINGFUL WORK

FAKE LAUGHTER

Ha. Ha. Ha.

A FAKE LAUGH AT YOUR BOSS'S LAME JOKE WILL EARN YOU POINTS

THE CRAMPED OFFICE SPACE

**MIGHT MAKE YOU ACCIDENTALLY TOUCH
FEET WITH YOUR DESK NEIGHBOUR**

PASSWORD MANAGEMENT

KEEPS ALL YOUR PASSWORDS IN A PLACE
WHERE THEY ARE EASY TO FIND

THE EMAIL FOLLOW-UP

YOU CAN SEND SOMEONE AN EMAIL AND
DO AN IN-PERSON FOLLOW-UP

OPEN OFFICE VIDEO CALLS

DON'T WORRY, YOU CAN TRUST YOUR COLLEAGUES WHO LISTEN IN ON YOUR VIDEO CALLS

VIDEO MEETING ROOMS

THERE ARE USUALLY PLENTY OF ROOMS
SUITABLE FOR VIDEO MEETINGS

TOILET PRIVACY

**WHAT HAPPENS IN THE TOILET
STAYS IN THE TOILET**

TEAM BUILDING

**YOU CAN DO CHALLENGING AND FUN
PHYSICAL ACTIVITIES TOGETHER**

THE SMELL OF FRESHLY BREWED COFFEE

THERE IS NOTHING LIKE PASSIVE COFFEE DRINKING

THE COFFEE MACHINE MINGLE

YOU WILL MEET A LOT OF COLLEAUGES AT THE
COFFEE MACHINE EAGER TO TALK TO YOU

THE CLIMATE CONTROL SYSTEM

ENJOY A NICELY VARIABLE INDOOR CLIMATE

THE ELEVATOR SILENCE

**TREATING COLLEAGUES AS PERFECT
STRANGERS REDUCES VIRUS SPREAD**

IMAGINARY DRAWING

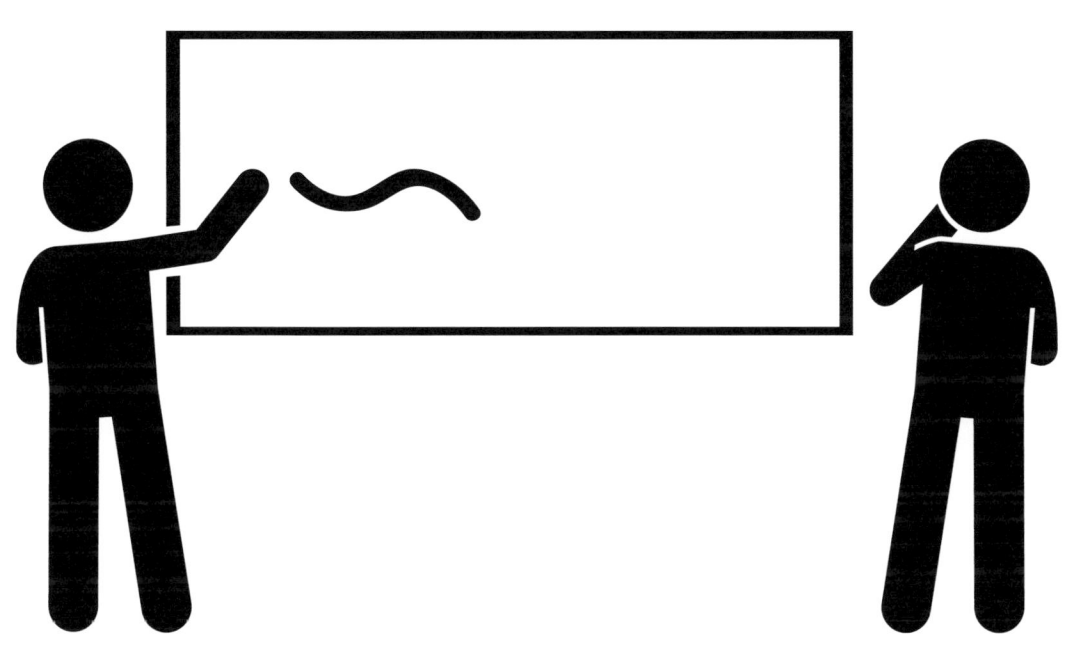

TAP INTO YOUR VIVID IMAGINATION WHEN ALL THE WHITEBOARD MARKERS ARE GONE

PERMANENT MARKERS

**HAVE FUN AT YOUR COLLEAGUES' EXPENSE
WITH PERMANENT MARKERS**

SPONTANEOUS SOCIAL INTERACTION

ENJOY SPONTANEOUS CHIT-CHAT
WITH YOUR COLLEAGUES

CORPORATE LINGO BINGO

PLAY FUN CORPORATE LINGO GAMES
WITH YOUR COLLEAGUES

THE PERSONAL COFFEE MUG

**AN EFFICIENT FORM OF TERRITORIAL PISSING
WHEN YOU LACK A PRIVATE OFFICE SPACE**

TIME FOR CONTEMPLATION

**WHEN YOU MISTAKE A VIDEO MEETING
FOR A PHYSICAL MEETING**

THE CONFERENCE TABLE

THANKS TO A REALLY LONG CONFERENCE TABLE NO ONE WILL QUESTION YOUR ABSOLUTE POWER

OFFICE INNOVATION

I call it "the wheel".
It's a decoration for barns.

**THERE IS NO BETTER PLACE TO THINK OUTSIDE THE BOX
AS BETWEEN FOUR WALLS (I.E. INSIDE A BOX)**

THE ANNUAL PERFORMANCE REVIEW

TOUCH BASE WITH YOUR BULLY FROM SCHOOL WHO IS IN CHARGE OF YOUR PERFORMANCE REVIEW

THE MEETING IN THE MEETING

YOU CAN HAVE YOUR OWN PHYSICAL MEETING
WITHIN A VIDEO MEETING

THE COFFEE BREAK

**WHEN FETCHING A COFFEE, MAKE SURE TO GET
A WORKOUT BY TAKING EVERYONE'S ORDER**

THE EMAILING DESK NEIGHBOUR

EMAIL YOUR DESK NEIGHBOUR WITHOUT SAYING ANYTHING TO CREATE AN AWKWARD MOMENT

THE WHITEBOARD DICTATOR

**MAKE SURE YOUR IDEAS WIN BY KEEPING EVERYBODY
AWAY FROM THE WHITEBOARD**

THE WHITEBOARD EUREKA MOMENT

TEARS OF JOY AS YOU FIND A WHITEBOARD
MARKER THAT ACTUALLY WORKS

OBLIGATORY FUN

THERE'S NO FUN LIKE OBLIGATORY FUN

OVERTIME

AN OPPORTUNITY TO FINISH THE WORK YOU DIDN'T DO DURING OFFICE HOURS

MULTIFUNCTIONAL SPACES

TAKE SOME REST AND CONTEMPLATE IN A SPACE WHERE YOU CAN ALSO FULFIL OTHER NEEDS

QUALITY TIME

AFTER A LONG DAY AT THE OFFICE YOU CAN LOOK FORWARD TO A LOVELY EVENING

A CASE OF THE MONDAYS

**A GREAT REASON TO CALL IN SICK AND WATCH
THE LATEST SEASON OF THE WHITE LOTUS**